# NO TIME TO WAIT

**Our story: God's purpose**

**By**

**Montel & Natalie Beecher**

Published by New Generation Publishing in 2022



First Edition



ISBN 978-1-80369-985-1

**www.newgeneration-publishing.com**

New Generation Publishing

# INTRODUCTION

Greetings to you in the precious name of the Lord Jesus Christ.

The reason why we have decided to write this book is because we believe in the importance of marriage and that marriage should be with someone who you can openly serve the Lord and Saviour Jesus Christ with.

Having said that, we also believe that the way relationships are approached within the church in modern society has become somewhat corrupted by worldly fantasies and lusts which not only have implications on the success of relationships but more importantly, they negatively impact your walk with Christ.

Through our own experiences and learning process, we know that God has revealed His perfect will to us through His Word so that we could be set free and share the truth with the generation of today. We decided that we do not want to allow any young person to experience the same things that we had to, neither do we want any soul to be lost trying to navigate their way through the whole "Godly dating" experience.

We pray that this book is not only a nice read for you, but that it creates a change in your thinking and provokes you to either make a change to your current situation, or that it will open your eyes to the unnecessary risks that we put ourselves at when we allow worldly doctrines to creep into the education of our saints. We pray that this book will help bring about revelation through the Word of God, thus, allowing you to walk into and through this stage of your life with your loins girt about with truth.

# CHAPTER 1- HOW WE MET

It all began on an early September's morning when both Natalie and I were invited to a youth event by a few of the youth leaders within the church that we were attending. Neither of us knew at the time that this was going to be the day that changed our lives completely as we knew it. In all honesty, neither one of us knew that the other person was even going to be at the event.

Montel's account

"I was just a young single guy who was trying to find his place in the church having recently committed to Christ, whilst also trying to ensure that I was ready for what was due to be my final year of studying for my degree at university. I had absolutely no intention of getting into any relationship and especially not at this point in my life. However, this was the first period in my life that I had completely surrendered my life to Christ, and I do believe that it was because my focus was on God and no longer on the things of this world such as relationships that meant that God saw the timing as correct for me to finally meet Natalie."

Natalie's account

"At this point in my life I was feeling quite distant from God but was trying to find my way back into a relationship with Him. I had decided to stay away from dating and focus on my university course and my relationship with Christ. Little did I know at the time, Montel would go on to become a huge part of that journey and in such a short amount of time also."

Now, what we have not yet mentioned was the fact that we had already been attending the same church for around 3 years prior to being introduced to each other. However, we had never held a conversation that was of any significance prior to the day of this youth event. For the record, our church was not one of those 20,000-seater megachurches where it is almost impossible to know every member that attends regularly. In fact, with only a couple hundred members at the church, it was probably easier to know everyone there than to not know them. Nevertheless, this period serves as a major indicator to us of just how intentional God is and how He really does have an appointed time set for ALL things.

And on the day of this youth event, it all changed. Again, without any expectation to see each other arrive at the pick-up location for this event, we both arrived amongst other young people. Unintentionally, we both sat right by each other both on the journey to the event and on the way back. We just seemed to gravitate towards each other spiritually and on a minibus that was full of young, excitable adults ranging from 16-30 years of age, all being deep in conversation, it really did feel as though the bus only carried the two of us as passengers. This was the gripping level of our conversation and instant connection after the first hello.

Whilst this was the first occasion that we did actually speak, this conversation, at the time of meeting, also served as confirmation from God of what He had shown to the both of us a long time before we actually met. Although neither of us would go on to reveal what it was that God actually showed to us until a much later date in the relationship.

**Montel's account**

"As previously stated, we had been attending the same church for the best part of 3 years and had never really previously spoken. However, from the very beginning God had drawn me to Natalie. Now, I know that this was God drawing me to her because in no way, shape or form was there ever any sexual desires or provocative thoughts towards her. I did not know anything about her or her family background, but spiritually I was drawn to her. I even found myself declaring to my mother at a church convention that

I knew who my future wife was going to be. And this was long before Natalie and I had ever been properly introduced.

What made this even more significant was, as previously mentioned, that I had only recently given my life to Christ when I actually met Natalie so throughout the majority of the 3 years of attending the same church prior to meeting her, I was not even saved. Because of this, I had no idea what this sense of being drawn to Natalie even meant. It was not something that I prayed about before being saved, nor was it something I ever acted upon. I did not know what to do so I just brushed it off at the time as maybe just being attracted to her but that also was not really the route that I wanted to go down at all. To be completely honest, I had been dating a girl from outside of my church during the 3 years prior to meeting Natalie so I was very worried about paying too much attention to this prompting. All this led to me really pushing this calling to the back of my mind. Little did I know, that whilst I was focussing on the here and now, God was trying to show me my future and I just did not see it.

Despite God showing me my future, I do believe that there is a reason why I could not obtain this promise and actually meet Natalie until I was in Christ myself and we were both running towards the same goal in the same direction. The simple fact is that our Heavenly Father loves all of His children unconditionally and protects His children. The Montel "before Christ" would never have been able to be beneficial for Natalie and so it was important that for us to inherit this promise, I first had to be fully surrendered to God Almighty myself. Still, now that the time had come and we had finally communicated, God reminded me how He had been showing me this for years and how now was in fact, the appointed time."

**Natalie's account**

"During the time that we attended the same church I would only ever see Montel in passing and the most we would say to each other was hello. I did not know much about him at all, or his family background, but what I did know was that quite a few of the young women in the church thought he was attractive and because of this I never really had any intentions of pursuing or making any moves towards him. Having been raised in church, I always knew that I would marry a man in Christ and always hoped that God would still make this possible for me even after stumbling in my relationship with Him. However, I got to a certain point in my life where I was convinced that this opportunity had disappeared for me. I could not see how this would ever be possible for me and almost completely gave up on the idea. I decided to just do all that I could do to get back into a place of fellowship with God from a dark place. But our story just shows how God is eternally faithful and reminds me every day how even in my lowest place, He never ever forgot about me. God's timing is purposed, and no man can disannul it."

Of course with this newly established bond, we were both excited and looking forward to seeing what fruit could grow out of it. This really was the beginning of a period of significant lessons that would go on to shape the course of our lives both individually and collectively forever but above all, we knew from the very beginning that God had purposed it for such a time as this.

# CHAPTER 2- WHAT HAPPENED NEXT?

At this time, being the private individuals that we both are, we tried our very best to keep the news of this bond within a limited circle for as long as possible as we had both seen in our lives how the involvement of others in any aspect of life is not always beneficial for those involved.

Unfortunately, it did not take long before what seemed like everyone that we knew had found out and the news spread like wildfire. However, at the time we were sort-of okay with certain people finding out because after all, we were young individuals trying to grow in Christ and were probably as equally yoked as you could possibly be when you consider the fact that we were pretty much at the same junction in our spiritual walk with Christ. Knowing this then, we believed that there was a lot to gain from having older and more experienced people to lean on and to receive support from as we embarked upon this journey.

Naturally, the news also began to circulate throughout the entire congregation of our church, and it was not long before we had many questions coming our way. We also had multiple people getting in contact with us to offer their services as "relationship counsellors" for us. Now, whilst we believe that the intentions were of good nature, in all honesty, it felt very pressurised. It felt as though other people saw this as an opportunity for them to have a success story if we were to go on and get married. However, this was not the attention that we were seeking nor expecting. In fact, all we wanted to do at this point was have the space to be able to get to know one another in a safe way and make sure that the foundations were right for us to build upon. Despite our intentions however, and after much negotiation between one another over the corresponding weeks, we decided that we would listen to the advice of others and go along with this whole "dating" thing. We decided that we would come to a decision in terms of who we would allow to be our "supervisors".

Now we do have to be honest and say that this was a very weird time for us. After listening to the ideas of numerous brethren and their plans, one thing that did strike us as quite worrying was how negative each person's view was in terms of dating "God's way". However, despite the negative outlook on it, the general consensus was that dating was definitely something that had to be endured.

## Montel's account

"I remember how one of the first things that was said to me left me feeling very conflicted. "Young man, this is going to be so hard for you guys and there is even more pressure on you Montel because you are the man". To be completely honest, my initial reaction was one of shock. Whilst I knew that Christ never promised any of us an easy life, I could not understand why this was the mindset towards something that had supposedly been approved of by God. I mean, if this is what every young/single person within the church is being taught from the beginning, is there any wonder why there are so many people looking to the world to find their life-partners? Imagine that, being told to walk down a certain path that will be nothing but a struggle and with no guarantee of any promise also. How encouraging is that?".

I think oftentimes, as believers, we forget that God really is the God of hope and whilst He certainly promises us trials in this world, He also instructs us to be of good cheer BECAUSE He has overcome the world. You see… HOPE! All this negative mindset did for us was drain the hope out of us.

Now, whilst we are sure that the idea at the time was not to try and stop either one of us from seeing each other, what we did realise was that there was a very pessimistic approach towards "dating" from the very beginning. It was almost as though the aim had been set to just try and help people survive this "impossible" period of dating as best as possible. Upon reflection, this should have acted as a major alarm bell to cast some serious doubts over the path we were about to be led down. Without a doubt God had brought us together, and so, in hindsight, finding out the path that He had set for His people should have been our first point of call. Unfortunately, being the inexperienced individuals that we were at the time, we were persuaded that because "dating" had been generally accepted in the church, it had to be God's plan for His children.

# CHAPTER 3 – THE COMMANDMENTS OF DATING

So, having made our decision on who we would allow to act as guidance for us during this new phase for both of our lives, we immediately received instructions on how we were meant to journey through this period.

1. "Thou shalt only gather in public places i.e., university library."
2. "Thou shalt not continue to be assembled together past the hour of 1900PM."
3. "Thou shalt not attend any romantic establishment such as a restaurant without a supervisor being present with thou."
4. "Thou shalt not sit any less than 3 cubits length away from each other."
5. "Thou shalt report back to thy supervisor informing them of whence thou went and what thou did after the completion of every gathering between the two of thou."

These are just some of the rules that were laid out for us to be able to navigate our way through "Godly dating" safely. Again, we want to reiterate that this is not an attack on anyone, but this is to show the kind of doctrine that is being taught to the young people of today. To be completely honest, it felt as though what had started out for us as an exciting opportunity to grow together in Christ had by now been turned in to just another one of those 'religious activities' forced upon people. We figured that the inclusion of these rules came with the expectation that under this kind of 24-hour surveillance there would be no opportunity for any kind of wrong-doing to occur. However, this was yet another striking alarm bell for us as we were, and even more so now are big believers that Christ Jesus is the answer in all things. And so, if all these rules were designed correctly to limit the risk of doing the wrong things, then surely God would back this up with His Word.

*"No temptation has overtaken you except such as is common to man; but God is faithful, who will not allow you to be tempted beyond what you are able, but with the temptation will also make the way of escape, that you may be able to bear it." 1st Corinthians 10:13. NKJV.*

So, we see here that God has already confirmed that no matter what challenge or temptation that we come across, He will make an escape for us so that we are able to withstand the pressure. What was striking to us at this time was that none of these rules that were so clearly developed by man were given to us with any kind of biblical foundation to attach it to. Remember, we had just been told on numerous occasions how tough this period was for anyone to bear, and so, if God truly desired for His people to even go down this route of "dating" then surely, He also would have ensured that He had clearly laid out the steps for us to be able to bear it and overcome this period of dating also. So why were these biblical proofs not provided? And if there were not any, what business did we have going down this route that was not ordained by God in the first place?

Please do not misunderstand us. Whilst these were some of the questions running through our mind at the time, it was evidently clear to see why these man-made rules were designed. These rules were created solely with the prevention of fornication in mind which we understood completely. However, what also became increasingly clear to us from that moment was that there is a lot more to this "Godly dating" culture that we had found ourselves in than was currently being revealed.

In truth, this did leave us with more questions than what we had originally started off with. On the one hand we had been forbidden from even going out for a meal without a 'supervisor', whilst on the other hand, we could not understand how we were expected to learn about each other and grow if every time we did meet up, there was someone else there acting as our mediator. How long were we expected to "date" like this before we could actually get to know one another? This was the confusion that we were left with.

Now, as a disclaimer, we would like to clarify that we knew and understood at that time that sex outside of marriage was and is not what God has intended for man and woman and is in fact a sin against God. Colossians 3:5-7 teaches us that fornication shall cause the wrath of God to come upon all the children of disobedience.

*"5Therefore put to death your members which are on earth: fornication, uncleanness, passion, evil desire, and covetousness, which is idolatry. 6Because of these things the wrath of God is coming upon the sons of disobedience, 7in which you yourselves once walked when you lived in them." Colossians 3:5-7. NKJV.*

There can therefore be absolutely no confusion left here at all on how God feels about fornication. Sex outside of marriage is wrong. However, and perhaps more to the point, if there were so many rules that had to be developed by man outside of God's Word to try and survive this period as gracefully as possible because of the temptations that it brings, then we also have to ask ourselves whether in fact "Godly dating" was ever something that God ordained for our lives in the first place, or, whether it was just another topic that had just become popular from a worldly standpoint and had worked its way into church doctrine.

Now, the following chapters are going to provide you with an insight into how the following months played out for us and how the experience of this period impacted our lives forever.

# CHAPTER 4- OUR EXPERIENCE

As stated in the previous chapter, we were given a list of man-made rules that we were told to stick to. What we realised through this period of "dating" was that whilst these rules and ideas were literally developed with the sole focus of preventing fornication, "dating" actually left the door open for other issues to creep into our relationship which caught us both unawares and unprepared. Before we knew it, we were judging the success of our relationship and its progress by the standard of "how long has it been since we last thought of each other in a sexual way?" or even judging the success of every time we met up by "did anything happen?". As you can imagine, this only made it more difficult for us in the stages of growing and just wanting to get to know each other better.

In addition, what we also found during this place of "do nots" was that whilst we were only focusing on the things that we could not do, we missed the opportunities for the things that we could do. We were so afraid of this thing called fornication and all it's devastating consequences that we began to hide ourselves away from each other so that the issue could not rise. This was dangerous territory for us. What we found here is that we were no longer trying to build upon the foundation of faith in Jesus Christ, but instead, when we did eventually meet up, we were just trying not to sin. This was like a trap for us as this shift had our minds focused upon the power of sin, meaning that we were left to constantly dwell on that very thing. Upon reflection, this period reminds us of what the apostle Paul was trying to teach the church.

*"But sin, taking opportunity by the commandment, produced in me all manner of evil desire. For apart from the law sin was dead." Romans 7:8. NKJV.*

Here and in the subsequent verses of romans chapter 7, the apostle Paul is teaching us that without the law sin had no authority. Though it existed, it had no authority. But what we see in verse 8 is that sin used the law to revive itself and cause man to fall. Once man had the knowledge of what sin was through the law, sin gained power. That's why the Word of God teaches us that the strength of sin is in fact the law. Now, to clarify, we are not comparing the rules of "dating" to the law of the covenant. However, what we are trying to show is that just as sin used the law as an opportunity to grow, so too has sin also used these rules that were developed by man and this period of dating to revive itself and bring about unfruitful desires.

*"For sin, taking occasion by the commandment, deceived me, and by it killed me." Romans 7:11. NKJV.*

This is where the issues crept in. You see, the law was not an evil thing. How could it be, God created it. However, sin used the law as an opportunity to gain power over the people because through the law came the knowledge of sin. And so, for as long as God's people remained under the law, sin would always have power over them. But this is why we Give glory unto our Lord Jesus Christ. As a result of sins deception, man needed a saviour to deliver us from the law. That deliverance came through the Lord Jesus Christ.

Now, notice what the apostle Paul goes on to teach us in verse 13 here…

*"Did that which is good [the law], then become death to me? Certainly not! But sin, in order that it might be revealed as sin, was producing death in me by [using] this good thing [as a weapon], so that through the commandment sin would become exceedingly sinful." Romans 7:13. AMP Bible.*

In the same way then as the law was not an evil thing, these man-made rules of dating also were not evil rules. However, what these "rules" do is give occasion to sin as they continue to place all focus upon sin which only gives opportunity to sin to deceive and destroy. Our minds were constantly thinking about the sin and all the dangers of it that we became imprisoned by it. And it absolutely did deceive us and destroy us.

Now, are we suggesting that the wrongs and rights should not be explained to all in pre-marital relationships? Not at all. However, we believe that the focus must be driven away from the pessimistic approach that magnifies the power of sin and shifted towards the victory that has been won through Jesus Christ for every single child of God and the desired goal which should always be the blessing of marriage that God has purposed for His children. Then, and only then, will two people walk with purpose towards that goal. Failure to do this will only allow sin to continue to lie and deceive people into allowing it to produce death in them, as we experienced all too well.

That being said, and having our minds solely fixated upon the power of sin, we were roped in. It got us, and we were devastated. What followed immediately after this was the unbearable weight of condemnation and this was not a good place for us to be at all. This was not what we wanted at the beginning, nor during any time of the relationship. Suddenly, we felt like we were in a never-ending cycle of trying to abstain and then falling off because of this condemnation. You see, whilst some outside of Christ may have their own personal reasons for wanting to abstain from sex outside of marriage, for believers it is simply a command and for good reason. For the both of us, this period represented some of the darkest days of our lives as it was more than just a personal choice that was destroyed, it was our walk with God that had been impacted. The truth is, unless you know what it truly means to be forgiven by God and why exactly He does forgive, it is so easy for condemnation to overtake you and weigh you down. And this is exactly what happened to us. The impact that this had on us was extremely negative and as we said, it led to some of the toughest times that either of us have experienced.

Now, some may be thinking “it was only sex... it happens!”. And for those people, we would like to share a passage with you.

*"21And you, who once were alienated and enemies in your mind by wicked works, yet now He has reconciled 22in the body of His flesh through death, to present you holy, and blameless, and above reproach in His sight—" Colossians 1:21-22. NKJV.*

Whilst this passage demonstrates the finished work of the Lord Jesus Christ on the cross to reconcile mankind unto the Father, we also see here how it is the wicked works of man (sin) that causes us to be separated from God. This evil behaviour is what causes you to be alienated and to become the enemies of God. Knowing this then, it is easy to understand how this level of self-condemnation that we experienced came about as at no point in either of our lives had we ever felt so distant from God. Not because God had removed Himself, but because we had sinned and could not look past how much we had failed. We felt that there was no way back at all. This heartbreak from feeling as though we had destroyed the good work that God had begun in our lives, suddenly became overwhelming.

We started avoiding each other and trying to not see each other for as long as possible because it felt like this was the only real way of ensuring that there was no room for bad thoughts or feelings. On the occasions that we did see each other, both of us were constantly treading on eggshells the whole time scared of making any mistakes. Before we knew it, things became hugely different. We were hiding away from each other in fear and this place of imprisonment started to not only affect us in our relationship and our walk with God, but it started to creep into our university studies also and even into our separate family lives as well.

**Montel's account**

"I just became very distracted in my studies during the first semester of my 3rd year at university to the point where I completely lost all motivation to carry on and was no longer attending my course. It was so bad that I had missed several deadlines for assignment due dates, and I was even threatened with being removed from the course as the university told me that it was looking likely that there would be no other option. I could not explain this place I was in, it just felt as though I had fallen into a dark hole and could not come out of it no matter what. I tried to get up and attend university, but it just would not happen. My mother was worried about me, but I never seemed to have the words that could describe what was happening. Something had to change and fast, otherwise, things were only going to end one way."

The truth is "dating" was not an enjoyable experience and although we had seen many people go through this route of "Godly dating", we really began to wonder how anyone would be able to continue dating for numerous years before marriage whilst seeing this conflict between spirit and flesh rage on. Nevertheless, we had seen many who claimed to be dating "God's way" endure long enough to make it unto marriage and after having experienced this thing ourselves first-hand, we were puzzled as to how. Was it only us who had experienced this struggle? or had the others just completely fallen into Ephesians 4:19 and given themselves over to these lusts without any battle? Had people just decided to struggle in silence because they believed it was the only way? How about those couples who did not survive until marriage? how different would the outcome of their time together have been if they were not constantly in a battle against these fleshly desires? So many questions that we just did not have the answers to.

However, one thing was for certain, we now understood why there was such a negative outlook on this phase of life that we are all made to feel like we must endure. At this moment in time, we had no idea what we found ourselves in, but surely this was not what God intended for His children, right?

# CHAPTER 5- WHAT CHANGED?

So, after trying everything that we could think of by ourselves, and after avoiding reading the bible because of our shame, one day we came to ourselves (sort of like the story of the prodigal son) and we decided that we could not keep running. We decided that we could no longer allow the self-condemnation to stop us from finding truth. We dusted off our bibles and chose to study for ourselves exactly what God had said, if anything, about "dating" and the challenges that we were facing. And what we found was incredible.

Now, we mentioned previously about the warfare that we experienced between our spirits and our flesh. It seemed like we knew what we ought to be doing but just could not seem to walk in it or move past this bondage. This is where the hidden issues became obvious for us and whilst we were directing our attention towards this warfare, the rest of our life was being brought to a standstill. What we discovered was that this is exactly what the apostle Paul warned the church in Galatia about. Galatians 5:16-17 teaches us that it is this warfare that prevents you from fulfilling anything in your life, especially the things that God has set out for you.

*"16I say then: Walk in the Spirit, and you shall not fulfil the lust of the flesh. 17For the flesh lusts against the Spirit, and the Spirit against the flesh; and these are contrary to one another, so that you do not do the things that you wish." Galatians 5:16-17. NKJV.*

This completely explained it. No wonder there was no progress happening for us in the relationship or in any other area of our lives. We were trapped and did not even realise it. Whilst this warfare is going on, it is true that you can make no progress. Therefore, it is important that we end this warfare by completely destroying any opportunity for the lusts of the flesh to arise.

Now, we know what you are thinking, "why would God have caused you to walk into a trap?". Good question. And the answer to that is simple, He didn't. Christ came to set the captives free. And so, the fact that we were in a place of bondage is evidence to show that this was not a place in our lives that had been ordained by God.

Furthermore, we also mentioned how overwhelming it all became. But again, we see that this is a complete contradiction to what the Word of God revealed to us. 1st Corinthians 10:13 teaches us that God does not allow you to be tempted by any temptation that will overcome you. In fact, God gives you a way of escape so that you can overcome it.

*"No temptation has overtaken you except such as is common to man; but God is faithful, who will not allow you to be tempted beyond what you are able, but with the temptation will also make the way of escape, that you may be able to bear it." 1st Corinthians 10:13. NKJV.*

Suddenly, it hit us. Not only did God not want us to be trapped by this thing, but He never ordained "Godly dating" in the first place. 1. God has instructed us to walk in the spirit and not after the flesh. So then why would God approve of anything that only intensifies the warfare between the two? 2. Dating is a place where temptations are undoubtedly given much room to grow. So then, if God provides a way of escape in all temptation, why would anyone persist with dating which only strengthens the issue and not look for the true way of escape that God has provided?

We pray that you understand that this deception was caused by the enemy himself and was exactly what he wanted to occur. We sinned, became trapped, felt defeated, condemned ourselves and ultimately hid ourselves away from God because of this guilt and shame. Tell us, does this not sound exactly like where the devil wants God's people to be? For you to feel so worthless that you cannot even see God's love anymore? Or, even worse, for you to die in that place of condemnation? This is why we are warned in 2nd

Corinthians 2: 11 to never be ignorant of the devils devices. Satan presents himself as an angel of light and tries to lure many in through nicely worded ideas but we as heirs of the promise of salvation, are not called to judge things by how they might seem but to judge them against the measure of God's Word.

*"Judge not according to the appearance, but judge righteous judgement." John 7:24. KJV.*

You see, before entering into anything, we are to judge it and see whether this thing is in line with God's Word or not. And if the answer is a negative, we have absolutely no business getting involved with it. It does not matter how much we try to spiritualise it or try and put the word "godly" before it, some things were just never meant for the church.

And since we are exposing the lies of the devil here, let us set some things straight.

*"The sting of death is sin; and the strength of sin is the law." 1st Corinthians 15:56. KJV.*

Understand that this life is a completely spiritual one, and death is a demonic spirit. And what this spirit does to attack you is try and hurt you with sin. This means that when sinful temptations come around you, it is not just that temptation that you are up against. In fact, there is a demonic spirit behind that sin trying to destroy you. Why is this important? Well, the bible also teaches us that the wage of sin is death which means that death knows that if it can get you to be overwhelmed by sin, then it has you right where it wants you, in death. By entering into "dating", you are entering into a place that keeps the temptation of sin close to you and continues to give room to death to try and sting you with sin. Remember how the apostle Paul warned us previously about sin in romans 7. The Word of God teaches us that sin uses the tactic of deception. And what is more is that the attack does not stop there.

*"10Now whom you forgive anything, I also forgive. For if indeed I have forgiven anything, I have forgiven that one for your sakes in the presence of Christ, 11lest Satan should*

*take advantage of us; for we are not ignorant of his devices." 2nd Corinthians 2:10-11. NKJV.*

Notice what the scripture has said here. The apostle Paul teaches us that the lack of forgiveness is actually a device used by the devil and affords him advantage over God's people. Whether you are the person who is not willing to offer forgiveness or the one who feels as though you can never be forgiven, the enemy uses this to bring overwhelming sorrow upon you. Now, this explains why after having messed up, we found it so difficult to even call on the name of the Lord Jesus Christ. We messed up, and could not see how we could ever be forgiven. Thus, drifting further away. This is why God makes it absolutely crystal clear in Ephesians 4:32 *"And be ye kind to one another, tender-hearted, forgiving one another, even as God for Christ's sake hath forgiven you". KJV.* You see, God does not want the devil to have advantage over anyone on this earth nor does he want anyone to become swallowed up with overbearing sorrow either. Therefore, God offers forgiveness to every repented heart on this planet through His Son Jesus Christ and instructs us to do the same.

What we saw in all of this is that this "Godly dating" movement is really just an opportunity for God's people to be defeated by Satan. The truth is, and as we previously mentioned, death uses sin to sting you by making you believe that sin has power. And this is where we were. We had not yet come to the revelation that we truly do have the victory over sin and death through the Lord Jesus Christ because by Him abolishing the law, He destroyed the strength of sin. Therefore, leaving death with no penetrable sting. You see, outside of this revelation, sin continues to deceive many. But when we understand the truth of God's Word, we no longer have to give any room to sin for us to battle against whilst believing that this is "just part of the journey". Instead, we can completely destroy all the devices of the enemy with the simplicity that is **IN** Christ.

Furthermore, the fact that mankind has deemed it necessary to create their own rules for heading into this period of "Godly dating" also highlights the lack of Gods approval for it and just how much we have over complicated our walk with Christ whilst attempting to be more acceptable for the world. But we have forgotten one crucial fact. The world is not trying to avoid fornication, they are promoting it. So then, when trying to achieve two completely contrasting outcomes, how have we opted to use the same method as the world? We really started to see how all this was wrong from the very beginning.

What we had realised as a result of all of this is that we had spent months engaged in an unnecessary, self-inflicted warfare and had ultimately been chained up because of it. This warfare led us to question whether God still had any plans for us on this earth after being under so much condemnation that we could not even bring ourselves to pray oftentimes. We realised that the reason that we were absolutely beaten down during this period and by this ideology was because it was not ordained by God at all. Thus, explaining why there are no biblical teachings on how to walk through "Godly dating".

But we thank God daily for His grace and His mercy. Because of His unfailing love, He brought us out of the grave and He opened our eyes to the blind deception that we had walked into and revealed the truth unto us, so that we may be set free.

*"1I love the LORD, because He has heard My voice and my supplications. 2Because He has inclined His ear to me, Therefore I will call upon Him as long as I live. 3The pains of death surrounded me, and the pangs of Sheol laid hold of me; I found trouble and sorrow. 4Then I called upon the name of the LORD: "O LORD, I implore You, deliver my soul!" 5Gracious is the LORD, and righteous; Yes, our God is merciful." Psalms 116:1-5. NKJV.*

And so, having been made aware of both where we were and how we got there, the only thing that there was left to know now was "how do we get out of here?".

# CHAPTER 6- DAY OF REVELATION

After months of being stuck under this chain and having become fed up and disheartened, we were left with questions such as "why would any child of God have to go through this kind of experience to receive God's gift of marriage?" Why is there so much stress attached to "dating" and especially when trying to do it "God's way?" "Is there something wrong with us?" "Could it be that there was just a genuine problem with us, and nobody else experienced these struggles?" Honestly, we thought we were cursed and no matter what we tried to do and all the rules that we tried to follow, there was just no breaking this hold. By this point, God had now revealed to us how this was never what He planned for His people at any point. So, how did we break free from this place?

Well, not many days after God showed us that this was never the place for us, we came together one night and as the key to any true breakthrough in life, we prayed. We fell to our knees and just spoke to God directly from the heart. "Lord, we do not know what to do. We cannot forget how it is you who has placed us together in the first place. But now we know that we were never supposed to go down this route and we are terribly sorry. Lord, now that we are here, how do we come out of this place?"

We do have to admit that at this point, it honestly seemed as though there was no other option than to give up and go our separate ways. Even though we now knew where we were and how we got there, it still did feel as though too much had happened to move forward. But then what would have been the necessity of meeting in the first place? Never mind all the months of challenges that occurred in our lives from that moment. We just knew that there was a purpose for ALL of this. Philippians 1:6 teaches us that our God is truly the God of completion.

*"I am convinced and confident of this very thing, that He who has begun a good work in you will [continue to] perfect and complete it until the day of Christ Jesus [the time of His return]." Philippians 1:6. AMP Bible.*

So, because we knew that it was God who began a good work and placed us together in the first place, we did not believe that giving up was the answer. Though many would have said at that time to call it a day, we just trusted God too much to give up completely without letting Him show it to us. There was no way all this was just an "experience". There had to be a purpose… Right?

Well, once we had prayed that evening, we felt led strongly by God to bible study together. This draw from the Holy Spirit was as though there was a necessity to be in the Word like never before. At first, we did not know where to begin so we spent a little time just looking through whilst trying to find a place to start. We went from Old Testament scriptures to New Testament scriptures just looking for a place to land and it was in this that we saw God completely answer our prayers in a supernatural way. It was as though a magnifying glass had been placed in front of our eyes and over a certain scripture and it caused the Word of God to pop out to us and pull us in like we had never experienced. And this really is where our whole lives changed completely.

*"1NOW concerning the things whereof ye wrote unto me: it is good for a man not to touch a woman. 2Nevertheless, to avoid fornication, let every man have his own wife, and let every woman have her own husband." 1st Corinthians 7:1-2. KJV.*

So there it was in all its boldness. The Word of God setting straight the path of those who believe. Here we see that the apostle Paul is confirming the sin that is fornication, and not only so, but Paul also reveals the very way that **GOD** Himself has set out for mankind to truly conquer this darkness… **MARRIAGE.** And it was at this moment that it all finally clicked for us. You see, God knew ahead of time that fornication would be a temptation in this world and so

He made sure (just as He promised) that He made that way of escape available for all to know. Notice, the apostle Paul said that to **AVOID** fornication, every man should have his own wife and vice-versa. Meaning, whilst mankind spends eternity trying to come up with new "ground-breaking" methods to try and minimise the threat of fornication inside of "Godly dating", our God has already delivered the knockout blow to sin. No longer can marriage just be seen as something that people do, or eventually do once they have had enough of dating. Instead, marriage has to be recognised as the very thing that God has given unto mankind to be an overcomer of the sins of this world.

Once again, we see that everything has been over-complicated in such a drastic way that has ultimately led to the downfall of many believers. We were handed several rules that, whilst they undoubtedly sounded great to those who come up with them, they were created by man for one reason only, and that was to try and stop the risk of fornication. But look at what GOD did. God had already declared the only rule that would completely shatter this element of darkness from your life **FOREVER**. He said, **"to avoid fornication... GET MARRIED!"**. The way that we were hoping God would make for us, He already made it and had indeed already spoken it!

Now, you may be saying "I could have told you that!" and whilst we do hope that this is something that is general knowledge within the body of Christ, we do however know that in modern society this is not the way we see things. And we shall discuss this further in the forthcoming chapters.

In returning to the day of this revelation, we suddenly felt like there was this overwhelming peace that came upon us both as we had finally found direction and realised the purpose behind our experience. God gave us this revelation that meant we could finally walk out of the bondage that we were in and truly walk into the freedom that Christ has called us into.

*"For you, my brothers, were called to freedom; only do not let your freedom become an opportunity for the sinful*

*nature (worldliness, selfishness), but through love serve and seek the best for one another." Galatians 5:13. AMP Bible.*

Being in Christ means that you have been brought into a life of freedom. But it is necessary to stress that the freedom does not mean to go and to do whatever you wish in a life that is not glorifying Jesus Christ. Rather, it means that if you follow Him wholly, then there is a true freedom that you shall enter into and obtain and use to bless others. We believe that God did not make us go through this experience, however, He allowed this experience so that through it we would seek Him, and He would show Himself to be our ever-present way maker. Freedom is in Christ, but it requires our obedience to His Word to inherit it.

## CHAPTER 7- SO WHAT DID WE DO?

Therefore, knowing the importance of obedience to God's Word, that is exactly what we did. We were obedient to the truth. Less than 1 month later we were engaged and were actively seeking the best way to get married. Suddenly, we were walking differently. Our focus shifted as we were no longer just trying to survive the duration of a relationship with fear, but now, having received truth, we had brought the relationship into alignment with God's will and made marriage the outcome. And we were pressing ahead.

Now, it is important to remember that we were young university students at this time and so money was not really something that we had in abundance which meant that we could not really entertain the idea of a sizeable wedding at that point. So, we decided to do things a little different to allow for no more delays. We decided that a registry office would be the best way for us to get married. Now, you are probably thinking. "Uhm, that is not glamourous at all!" and of course, we could have delayed it and waited until we had saved up more money so that we could have splashed out on the big day. But the truth is, we chose to sacrifice all that external stuff for our own salvation.

*"24Do you not know that in a race all the runners run [their very best to win], but only one receives the prize? Run [your race] in such a way that you may seize the prize and make it yours! 25Now every athlete who [goes into training and] competes in the games is disciplined and exercises self-control in all things. They do it to win a crown that withers, but we [do it to receive] an imperishable [crown that cannot wither]. 1st Corinthians 9:24-25. Amp Bible.*

You see, when we see Olympic sprinters competing in their races, they all run with their focus on the gold medal. They know that whilst there are 3 medals available, the only true satisfaction is the gold medal, and that prize lies ahead of them all but only one person can receive it. Now, whilst salvation and the promise of eternal life is available for all, we are to run with that same vigour and determination to obtain the incorruptible reward that is set before us. This means that we are to run with focus and not allow ourselves to be slowed down by the corruptible things of this world. Whilst a big wedding is great, is it worth your victory and freedom?

In addition to this victory and freedom that awaited us on the other side of obedience, 1st Corinthians 7:9 also teaches us that it is a better thing for the unmarried to get married than to burn because of sexual immorality.

*"But if they cannot contain, let them marry: for it is better to marry than to burn." 1 Corinthians 7:9. KJV.*

Admittedly, we spent some time in this trap of deception and destruction which meant that this was a decision that we had to make. We had the option to either end this warfare between spirit and flesh right now and **DO** the will of God or, we could have delayed it until we found that all the worldly desires were in place i.e., big wedding, money saved up to buy our first house, career established etc. but then what state would we have found ourselves in? Where would placing God's will behind our own will leave us? The bible teaches us that it is our responsibility as children of God to serve God with Godly fear and it was this truth that made our decision a lot easier. After all, tomorrow really is never promised.

*"28Therefore, since we are receiving a kingdom which cannot be shaken, let us have grace, by which we may serve God acceptably with reverence and godly fear. 29For our God is a consuming fire." Hebrews 12:28-29. NKJV.*

Finally, and most importantly, Jesus Christ teaches us exactly what kind of person can and cannot be His disciple. The words of Jesus Christ have been highlighted in the passage below for the purpose of understanding.

*"24Then Jesus said to His disciples, "if anyone wishes to follow Me [as My disciple], he must deny himself [set aside selfish interests], and take up his cross [expressing a*

*willingness to endure whatever may come] and follow Me [believing in Me, conforming to My example in living and, if need be, suffering or perhaps dying because of faith in Me]. 25For whoever wishes to save his life [in this world] will [eventually] lose it [through death], but whoever loses his life [in this world] for My sake will find it [that is, life with Me for all eternity]. 26For what will it profit a man if he gains the whole world [wealth, fame, success], but forfeits his soul? Or what will a man give in exchange for his soul?" Matthew 16:24-26. AMP Bible.*

There we have it. Chasing after the things that the world teaches you to desire before it is acceptable for you to get married will cause many to lose their life because of that warfare between the spirit and flesh which, as previously stated, stops you from doing the things which you ought to be doing and as the apostle Paul said, causes you to burn. Thus, meaning that you can never truly come to the place of following after Christ. What would happen if you found yourself standing before the king of glory whilst stuck in that warfare? Is it worth your soul? This is why the Lord Jesus Christ said that you have to be prepared to deny yourself (your will, your desires) in order to truly follow after Him. We were not prepared to stand before Christ and tell Him that the reason we were not obedient to His will is because we felt as though we needed to have the things of this world first. Salvation was and is for us the most important thing out of it all. After all, is this not what salvation is all about?

*"11For the [remarkable, undeserved] grace of God that brings salvation has appeared to all men. 12It teaches us to reject ungodliness and worldly (immoral) desires, and to live sensible, upright, and godly lives [with a purpose that reflect spiritual maturity] in this present age," Titus 2:11-12. Amp Bible.*

That being said, we booked the registry immediately. Now, the challenge that presented itself at this time was that the earliest availability that they had at that time was 4 months away from the date in which we were engaged. At first, we were disappointed that we would have to wait so long, but once we were reminded of the freedom awaiting us, we knew that this was the perfect opportunity to conquer this warfare by walking boldly and strongly toward our victory. We could finally see the light at the end of this particularly challenging tunnel. In this time, we saw how having the goal set before us completely changed our mindsets and allowed us to walk so much stronger even before the marriage because we knew that we had obeyed the voice of God and were about to enter all that He had planned for us.

It is also necessary for us to mention that we did not tell a single person about the decision that we had made. As we have mentioned, we knew that we were walking by faith alone and we were careful not to allow carnal minds to distract us away from this enormous opportunity. Now, when applying for a registry office wedding, it was required for us to have our names displayed on a screen monitor at that registry office (which was also the office for all the city council dealings) for around 30 days to give anyone who knew us (and with a valid reason) the opportunity to object the plans for marriage. This was a particularly tough period for us as throughout our relationship prior to marriage, we faced a lot of backlash from certain groups of people who really hated the idea of us being together and tried to do everything that they could to create a lot of trouble for us. Because of this, we knew that if we did tell anyone, and the information had made its way back to these people, they would have made up any reason they could to attempt to sabotage our plans. And being completely honest, we were just not prepared to take that risk.

Secondly, we also knew that what we were doing was not something we could expect much support for at all. As we said, we knew what God had placed in our hearts and we did not want any external influence telling us how much of a risk it all is and how it will not work out etc. In truth, we chose to hear the report of the Lord and focus on God's Word alone. Because of this, our own mothers did not even know that we were even engaged until a few weeks prior to the big day! (Try hiding something so enormously life-changing from a mother who knows you inside-out...).

Anyway, fast-forward to the big day and we did it. Despite the fact that Montel was late (some things never change), we exchanged vows and had our mothers as witnesses and officially became husband and wife. By God's grace we were able to fly away a day or two later and enjoy a very eventful honeymoon knowing that we had just stepped into the beginning of the rest of our lives. No more bondage. The captives had officially stepped in freedom by the Word of God.

**Montel's account**

"I have never told Natalie this but there is one particular moment that occurred in the build-up to our wedding that has always and will always remain with me for all of my days and whenever the challenges of life come our way, I always remember this one thing. We were talking on the phone about this big decision that we were about to walk into and with me being my usual playful self, I made the comment that once we said the famous "I do", I would no longer be a free man. And it was her response that gave me even more confidence that this was 100% only going to be blessed by God. She said, "this is not the end of your freedom, it is the beginning of it for the both of us". At this moment, I knew that after everything that we had been through together, there was nothing that could ever separate the two of us."

# CHAPTER 8- HOW GOD BLESSED OUR OBEDIENCE

Now, we mentioned previously how we were young university students with no real money to our names at the time of marriage. Due to this, we went into the marriage without having any place secured to call our home. In addition to this, Montel had still not completed his 3rd year of university yet which meant that a full-time job was still not an option. Knowing this however, we chose to look past these circumstances and be obedient to God's Word in faith. Although we did not have the physical evidence yet, we trusted God and knew that we would see His blessing over our marriage. More importantly though, we knew that the eternal reward for obedience through faith in the Word of God was greater than any difficult period we may have to endure throughout the early stages of our marriage.

And so, to begin, we feel that it is important to mention that we were married for around seven months before we had our first place to live together. This is just to show you the kind of sacrifice that we were willing to make knowing that we were walking into freedom. When we first decided to get married, we knew that we would have to spend the beginning of our marriage apart, but in all honesty, neither of us foresaw having to endure this period for quite so long. We spent these 7 months living at our own family homes and just to put that into perspective, our families are from different cities which meant that visitations were never just spontaneous, but they had to be planned well in advance. Thus, leading to further limits on time spent together.

Did this period come with challenges? Of course, it was extremely difficult. They say that long-distance relationships do not work but that is nothing compared to a long-distance marriage. Remember, this was all during the year of university that we had entered so there were weeks without seeing each other and very little privacy available to us. This oftentimes led to the marriage being restricted to text messages and phone calls if possible. Though this period was not without its challenges, we still knew that this was all necessary. Not only for our salvation, but for our faith also because we knew that when we did see the glory of God in our marriage, we would have our testimony and our faith would be built even stronger.

"*And we know that all things work together for good to them that love God, to them who are the called according to his purpose.*" *Romans 8: 28. KJV.*

Now that we have given you a brief insight into the early stages of our marriage, we can begin to testify about the goodness of God in our marriage.

During the second semester of Montel's 3rd year of university, there was a lot of catching up to do as he completely missed the first semester due in main part to the issues previously explained in chapter 4. Considering the dissertation module and the 5 assignments missed during the first semester, and add to that the 5 other second semester assignments also, that left Montel with a total of 12 assignments to complete in less than 12 weeks. To say that this task seemed impossible for us at the time would be an understatement, but we can truly declare that what is impossible with man is always possible with God. From Montel being woken up in the middle of the night by a dream whereby God revealed his dissertation topic unto him without any previous consultation with any lecturer, to God providing Montel with the wisdom to know the exact topics to revise ahead of the final exam, the way God alone brought us through this semester to be able to complete university with a degree is worthy of all praise! (But this is a testimony to be saved for another book). We feel led to share how God supernaturally opened a window of opportunity for us as a family before Montel had even finished his dissertation.

Throughout studying at university, Montel had been working in a part-time capacity job for nearly 3 years to allow for time to study. In what seemed at the time to be completely out of the blue, and literally a day after Montel had completed his last module assignment and was due to start the type up of his 10,000-word dissertation, he received an email from his then-current employers threatening to terminate his contract of employment. Of course this was very worrying at the time as we were still not living together, and we still had no place to call our home yet so although Montel was getting through his university assignments, it felt like a major setback. The truth is the company wrongly accused Montel which they later admitted to and apologised for, but it was in this massive shake-up that we saw just how God is able to do that which surpasses abundantly above all that we ask or think.

Initially, after spending several months and weeks completing assignment after assignment, we were both looking forward to that moment where Montel could rest and take a break from academic chores. But having received this email, we knew that God was showing us that this was not the time to rest and in fact God had better waiting for us, so we needed to keep pushing. Even though the company retracted and apologised and did not fire him, the time spent in-between not knowing what was going to happen with the job gave Montel the boost that was needed to begin looking and applying for full-time job opportunities for life after university. Montel spent the next few days applying for every job opportunity that he came across whilst also working on his dissertation.

Now before we go any further, we want to stress that it is very true that many new graduates struggle to find a job upon graduation regardless of their results, and it is even more of a struggle to secure one before even submitting all of your assignments. Add to that the fact that Montel was almost kicked out of university during the first semester of his 3rd year due to falling so far behind with the workload and a lack of attendance, you will be able to see how God truly did show up for us in a miraculous way.

What God showed us in this time was that He really is our provider and although we did not see beforehand how things were necessarily going to come together, He showed us that His Word will never fail. The very first company that Montel applied for got back to him within a matter of days. And from here, God completely took us from glory to glory.

**Montel's account**

"Never before in my life had I been involved in a recruitment process that required you to go through 5 different stages before finding out whether you were successful or not. This was insane to me, but it was more than necessary. I remember going through the first 4 stages and whilst being extremely nervous, I prayed before heading into each one as I knew that God has the final say. From visiting the business during operating hours to face-to-face interviews, I was able to sail through all 4 of these stages with a lot of ease and my confidence just grew more and more. However, there was still one more stage to go through and stage 5 really did me catch me off guard. A few days prior to stage 5, I found out that the whole phase was a "day in the role" assessment centre. In all honesty, I had never even heard of an assessment centre before this, never mind participating in one. Now, what made this assessment centre even more daunting for me was the fact that I was being tested on various operational aspects of running a business which was a completely different world to what I was used to. I am a sport-science graduate.

Even to this day, I remember when I arrived at the assessment centre location and I saw all the other applicants sitting there. My heart fell into my stomach. I was not expecting to see anyone else there on the day, so this threw me off even more. I was just full of panic now. I remember going to the toilets to pray before the testing began but strangely, even after praying there was still that feeling of my stomach being a nest for a family of butterflies, and it was evident. From the beginning of the testing to the very end of it I barely spoke a word. It was as if there was a language barrier and I just could not seem to form any words that added any substance to the group discussions. Not wanting to embarrass myself or show how out of my depth I was regarding these tests, I chose to remain quiet. In hindsight, I see how fear had crept in and found a home.

Thankfully, there was an end to the group tests and with it came time for all applicants to individually sit in front of the assessors to be "questioned" in what felt more like a police interrogation. Honestly, I knew that the only chance I would have of even keeping alive the hopes of being successful in getting the job became dependent on this one interview. Knowing what this job could mean for me and my wife in terms of being a springboard for other opportunities such as having a home, there was no way that I could just head into it without the peace of God, so again I prayed before heading into the interview. I prayed that God would just direct my words and keep me calm and composed whilst also just thanking Him for bringing me this far knowing He is faithful to complete His work. After spending much of the day in hiding, only God could still turn this into a positive. And that is exactly what He did. He directed my words, and I came out of that interview knowing that I laid it all out there. And at the end of 8 hours of being tested, it was finally time to go home and I was told that I would find out if I had been successful or not over the next few days.

It was very weird actually. On my way home, and even after I reached my house, the only thing I could think about was how bad my performance was prior to that final interview. Even though I had left the assessment centre ultimately feeling positive because of the final interview, it was as though the only thing I could remember was the negative way in which the day began. My mom and my wife were asking me questions about it and I could not even bring myself to speak about it. I remember that evening deciding to build a wardrobe, just to take my mind off of it. Once the next morning came, I received a phone call from an unknown number which I missed. I knew immediately that it was from the company and I really did not want to call back. As soon as I saw their call, my mind automatically went back to all the things that went wrong throughout the whole day whilst pushing out the one aspect that went well. I was afraid, and to be honest, it was my mother who made me pick up the phone and call them back. To this day I am so grateful that she did.

The first thing the recruiter told me on the phone was that she and everybody else could see how nervous I was on the day, and how I hid myself away. Suddenly, the moment that I was afraid of seemed to be happening. But God. In what seemed like the same sentence, she said something that took me back completely. She told me that she had been speaking to one of the assessors who interviewed me, and that the assessor wanted to take a chance on me despite my performance at the beginning of the assessment. She said that the assessor was willing to take a chance on me because she saw something special in me during that final interview. At that moment I remembered how God had His hand over me that day and showed me that even when all hope seems to be lost, He is able. What was impossible for me, was always possible for God. On that day, I learned the most important lesson from God that has stuck with me all the days of my life. I was shown that it is not by my own strength that I was able to have overall success in the interview, but by God's grace and supernatural ability and there is no one who can ever take that away from me. Glory to God."

*"And you shall remember the LORD your God, for it is He who gives you power to get wealth, that He may establish His covenant which He swore to your fathers, as it is this day." Deuteronomy 8:18. NKJV.*

Once we received this news, we really did waste no time in looking for our first home together and we thank God because we found one not too long after Montel had started the job. This was amazing and even though we had already been married for several months prior, this really did feel like the beginning of our marriage all over again and the realisation of the thing that we had been hoping for with confident assurance. The job came 4 months after marriage, and our first home came 3 months after that. God blessed us with a wonderful home for our family that we could call ours and where we could raise our children. Now we never look back, only to give Him praise and glory! He saved us. He took us out of darkness and into His marvellous light. His perfect plan was complete.

*"29And seek not ye what ye shall eat, or what ye shall drink, neither be ye of doubtful mind. For all these things do the nations of the world seek after: and your Father knoweth that ye have need of these things. 31But rather seek ye the kingdom of God; and all these things shall be added unto you. 32Fear not, little flock; for it is your Father's good pleasure to give you the kingdom." Luke 12:29-32. KJV.*

You see folks, what started out with simple obedience to His Word, without having all the other things already in place, ended in victory in Christ Jesus. We believe that God is calling His people in these last days to let go of all the external cares and pleasures of this life because these are the very things that cause you to not see the glory of God. He said that **HIS** strength is made perfect IN weakness! We have to allow ourselves to be in positions of vulnerability where we have no choice but to trust Him completely if we are to ever see the true power of Christ rest upon us. When we place our focus upon the kingdom of God, **EVERYTHING** that we need shall be taken care of. Why? Because it is **HIS** good pleasure to give His children the kingdom. Jesus Christ showed us that He truly is the way, and we can say that we know Him to be so very true and loving. This really was the start of many more miracles that God has worked in our lives both collectively and personally since marriage that remind us daily that He has already placed His stamp of approval on our obedience to His word.

# CHAPTER 9- THE DANGERS OF "GODLY DATING"

Now that we have given you an insight into our story and our experience of "Godly-dating", we want to share our concerns for the generation of today who are more than ever finding themselves following the direction of worldly influences in favour of going down the route of "Godly dating" to be able to achieve the desires of this world first. Whilst there is absolutely no issue with having dreams that you would like to achieve within your lifetime, we do have to ask ourselves the question... "What price am I willing to pay for it?". Remember Jesus Christ Himself said that there is no gain for a person who achieves everything but has sacrificed their soul as a result of that. The truth is that the order in which we aim to achieve things has been turned upside down by the world and the church has allowed it to distract away from the truth and simplicity found in the Word of God.

*"31Therefore take no thought, saying, what shall we eat? Or, what shall we drink? Or, wherewithal shall we be clothed? 32(For after these things do the gentiles seek:) for your heavenly Father knoweth that ye have need of all these things. 33But seek ye first the kingdom of God, and his righteousness; and all these things shall be added unto you"*. Matthew 6: 31-33. KJV.

You see, as alluded to in the previous chapter, this divine order has already been set for us by Christ Himself ahead of time. Notice that according to the gospel of Matthew, not only are we called to seek the kingdom of God and His righteousness, but we are called to place our focus upon the kingdom of God **FIRST** before any other thing. God has promised that all other things shall be added unto you, but He has of a certainty given unto us an order to follow if we are to see these blessings of God manifest in our lives. Now think about it. What greater security is there than knowing that you have a promise made by the God for whom it is impossible to lie supporting you as you follow the path laid out in The Word? When we allow ourselves to seek first "all these things" we are actually causing the kingdom of God and His righteousness to become of secondary importance to us, thus, stepping out of His divine order. Dating, by its design, encourages the hushing of kingdom matters in favour of pursuing those other things. We, as believers, cannot allow this order to be tampered with because it has been set to make the crooked paths straight and without this we allow for the demise of our brethren as outside of God's plan for mankind, there is only destruction.

Now, why do you think that you will not find the concept of "Godly dating" or even "dating" alone in the bible at any point? God promised that there is no temptation that we can face that is not common to man so it can't be a new thing, right? So where did it come from? Well, let's see.

*"3But I am afraid that, even as the serpent beguiled Eve by his cunning, your minds may be corrupted and led away from the simplicity of [your sincere and] pure devotion to Christ. 4For [you seem willing to allow it] if one comes and preaches another Jesus whom we have not preached, or if you receive a different spirit from the one you received, or a different gospel from the one you accepted. You tolerate all this beautifully [welcoming the deception]. 2nd Corinthians 11:3-4. Amp Bible.*

This was the apostle Paul's deep worry from the very beginning of the churches existence. That the church would allow Satan to prize us away from the extremely simple truth that is found in Christ in favour of a more complicated and "self-fulfilling" Christian message. Unfortunately, this is exactly what has occurred. Now we find the world teaching the church the concept of 'dating' when it should have been the church teaching those in darkness what to do when blessed enough to find their life partner. Scriptures teach us that the way of this world follows after "the prince of the power of the air" and so there can be no surprise that this path only leads to a time of warfare and bondage for God's people. This is further evidence that God did not set the path for us so that He could just be strict, but He did it for our own protection.

Furthermore, look at what the apostle Paul said. He said that if any person comes along preaching another Jesus, another spirit, or another gospel to that which was originally preached, this person is corrupting the minds of the hearers and leading them away from the simplicity of Christ. So, does "Godly dating" preach a different message to the simple truth of Christ? Well, according to 1st Corinthians 7:2, marriage is the only true way to completely conquer fornication. According to "Godly dating", there are several methods that are available to try and help you avoid fornication. The issue with this is that these methods keep you in that place of dating without ever actually being able to completely close the door on it. This shows that there is an undeniable contrast between truth and theory. Dating has entered the church through deception. As the dearly beloved, we have to purposefully seek truth over nice sounding ideas.

*"And do not be conformed to the world [any longer with its superficial values and customs], but be transformed and progressively changed [as you mature spiritually] by the renewing of your mind [focusing on godly values and ethical attitudes], so that you may prove [for yourselves] what the will of God is, that which is good and acceptable and perfect [in His plan and purpose for you]." Romans 12:2. Amp Bible.*

You see, somewhere down the line it has been forgotten that God really does work ALL things in line with the counsel of His own will and has therefore instructed His children to be changed by the renewing of their mind. This means that there was once a way that we walked before accepting Christ, but now that we are **IN** Christ, there is a new way to follow. We have newness of life to walk in. God through Christ Jesus has made it available for us to both know His will and be transformed by it so that we as His children can walk in His purpose for our lives. Unfortunately, instead of walking in this purpose, many, like ourselves, have chosen to enter into a time of frustration and complications. Ultimately, you can always identify a lie from the truth when that fake truth starts to become complicated or confusing.

And lastly, we would like to highlight a further issue with the concept of dating by referring back to the point made during the sharing of our testimony. As we explained, Godly dating teaches man to develop numerous measures to try and avoid the risk of sexual immorality. The issue with this is that whilst these measures are being developed, the whole concept itself keeps you in a trap whereby the lusts and temptations of dating are forever lingering. Whether you go for a meal, watch a movie, or even talk on the phone, there is always opportunity for these things to creep in. For all these efforts made to avoid sin, you never truly shut the door completely away from these lusts whilst in a place of dating. This means that there is never any true place of peace during this time and because of this, it is important to note that what "Godly dating" fails to teach you is that the physical act is not where the issues begin in the first place.

*"14But every man is tempted, when he is drawn away of his own lust, and enticed. 15Then when lust hath conceived: it bringeth forth sin: and sin, when it is finished, bringeth forth death". James 1:14-15. KJV.*

According to the Word of God, temptation is a result of being drawn away by your own lust which if given opportunity to grow, brings forth sin, which in turns brings forth death. So, whilst the doctrine of 'Godly dating' teaches you to not physically do anything, oftentimes, the very thought that passes through your mind is the place where the problems arise. Now can you see the warfare that we explained earlier? You might feel good one day because you have not physically given in to these lusts, but there is no victory to celebrate because the warfare is still alive and is just as prevalent tomorrow. For as long as you keep yourself and your partner in a place of dating, regardless of how many supervisors you have or how far you sit apart in a restaurant, you will always remain vulnerable to these lusts warring against you which explains why the door of opportunity is constantly left open for sin to be brought forth throughout. This is otherwise known as bondage.

Now we can begin to see why the apostle Paul said, “to avoid fornication… **get married!**”. The amplified bible reads *“But because of [the temptation to participate in] sexual immorality, let each man have his own wife”*. That temptation to participate in sexual immorality is never truly conquered unless we end this bondage and completely slam the door of opportunity for sin to arise shut by coming out of dating and entering into marriage. This is great news isn’t it? Surely as believers we should want to remove any opportunity for lust to bring forth sin in our lives, Right? This is why we have the Word of God.

## Chapter 10- THE ALTERNATIVE?

Now, apart from the obvious alternative which is to follow after the sinful flesh which in turn only leads to eternal damnation, is there any other way? Can mankind really devise a good enough plan for "dating" that means you can do so without ever having these desires towards the person of the opposite sex? The truth is, no they cannot.

And here is why.

*"27So God created man in His own image, in the image of God created He him; male and female created He them. 28And God blessed them, and God said unto them, Be fruitful, and multiply, and replenish the earth, and subdue it: and have dominion over the fish of the sea, and over the fowl of the air, and over every living thing that moveth upon the earth." Genesis 1:27-28. KJV.*

Let us look at this. So, we see here in Genesis chapter 1 that God created the male and female inner man (the spirit) after His image and gave immediate instructions to His creation. This means that the very first instruction that came from God to His creation of mankind at the beginning of time was to bring forth fruit, become many, fill the earth, and dominate the earth. Notice the scripture teaches us that God blessed "them" and gave this instruction unto "them". Who is "them"? The male and female that He created. This means that this instruction was designed for the male and female to achieve **together**. In this very commandment we can see that God established the spiritual connection between both male and female from the offset for the purpose of this instruction. Thus, meaning that male and female were created to dwell together and work together from the beginning of creation. And it did not stop here either.

Genesis chapter 2 teaches us that God saw on the earth that it was not a good thing for the physical male to be alone.

And having called forth every animal that He had created for Adam to name them, God found that there was still no suitable helper that was found for Adam to look after the earth.

*"21And the LORD God caused a deep sleep to fall upon Adam, and he slept: and he took one of his ribs, and closed up the flesh instead thereof; 22And the rib, which the LORD had taken from man, made he a woman, and brought her unto the man. 23And Adam said, This is now bone of my bones, and flesh of my flesh: she shall be called Woman, because she was taken out of Man. 24Therefore shall a man leave his father and his mother, and cleave unto his wife: and they shall be one flesh". Genesis 2:21-24. KJV.*

WOW. Are we seeing it yet?

Not only did God establish the spiritual connection between both male and female at the beginning of time, but God also went that bit further and established the physical connection between male and female also. God caused a deep sleep to fall upon Adam, took one of His ribs and created a woman. You see, by God forming the woman out of the rib of the man and calling her to be the suitable helper that God intended for the male, He also established the eternal physical connection between male and female also. And now, because God really does work all things according to the purpose of His own will, by God's special design, it is both man and woman's nature to connect to one another and become one.

What's more, Jesus Christ Himself also confirmed the importance of the connection between male and female also.

*"But from the beginning of the creation God **MADE THEM MALE AND FEMALE**". Mark 10:6. KJV.*

Now, for the purpose of context, it is important to note that Jesus Christ said this in response to being asked a question about the lawfulness of divorce. In saying that "from the beginning of creation God made them male and female", Christ is not just merely stating the fact of God's creation, but He is demonstrating the manner in which mankind was created. God did not just create the female. God did not just create the male. God created them male AND female. Christ is answering the question on the lawfulness of divorce by highlighting the significance of remembering how we were created in the first place. **TOGETHER!** There is an inseparable nature in which God has designed for the male and female to function on this earth with. Praise the Lord!

So, what does this mean? Well, what this shows us is that by entering into "Godly dating", and by developing these man-made rules, mankind (the creation) is actually trying to achieve something that was never intended for us by our creator. How can we practise the idea of dating and not be drawn to the other person? It is our very nature to be drawn to the opposite sex which means that it is impossible for one to "date" a person of the opposite sex and never feel that physical connection towards them. And accepting this is okay. After all, this is the very reason why God has given unto man the gift of marriage long before we ever realised that we needed it.

As you can see, marriage is **NOT** a concept that scientists or other worldly influencers have developed nor have authority over. Instead, it is the very purpose of God for His creation of mankind. "Godly dating" and all the "relationship goals" that come with it has worked its way into the minds of the people and deceived the church to believe that we can somehow stop God's intention for mankind in favour of following the world's pathway. The two cannot work together. And the truth is, the only true relationship goal that we should ever have is marriage.

When we choose to go through the period of dating, we open many windows of opportunity for the chains of this world to try and grab a hold and we become enslaved. It does not matter what methods are created by human hands to try and make the pathway a little less crooked. Until we understand what is intended for us by God in relation to your life partner, the pathway will never be that simple, straight path that is found in Christ Jesus.

Ultimately, “Godly dating” in its simplest form, is placing yourself in a worldly position and then blaming God when it does not work out.

*“Neither give place to the devil”. Ephesians 4:27. KJV.*

# CHAPTER 11- SO WHAT IS THE UNDISPUTED TRUTH?

Now, we know what you are thinking... "you guys have already said it so many times… marriage!". And yes, whilst we have said this many times, the truth is that it really is that simple. We are in a society today where the whole world is running around looking for an answer to all these various situations that God has already determined. Remember the Lord Jesus Christ said, "I am the way, the truth and the life". He did not tell us that He would try to find a way for us or find a solution, but He made it clear that from the very beginning until the very end of time, there has and will only ever be one truth: The Word of God. All truth is found in Him. Therefore, as children of the one true and Holy God, we must learn to put an end to endless dating.

You see, when we enter into relationships with no actual goal set before us in terms of marriage, we fall into that place of "seeing how it goes" which really is the beginning of a steep downhill fall. Your focus is on your personal desires e.g., money and the affairs of this life rather than positioning yourself in a place of obedience.

*"Therefore shall a man leave his father and his mother, and shall cleave unto his wife: and they shall be one flesh". Genesis 2: 24. KJV.*

The bible teaches us that when the two separate parts join together in marriage, they shall begin to be one flesh. There is a true blessedness about this as God is showing us that as the two become one, not only are the two meant to just come together, but they are called to grow together and achieve together and be inseparable in **all** things. Life now becomes a "together journey" which also helps us to understand why God gave the instructions of mankind's role on this earth to both the male and female. God wants us to achieve **together**. This means that you help build each other to achieve all your dreams and grow in what Christ Jesus has set out for you **together**. Isn't this just amazing? Look at God's intended plan! Imagine being able to look back in the years down the line and see everything that you have built together! You see, there really is no reason for any person to allow their "goals" to hold them back from marriage as God intended for it to be able to give birth to those dreams and visions. Once we come to an understanding of this, we can remove the time wasted on all things unnecessary.

Additionally, as believers we must remember what the victory that Christ won for us on the cross actually means for us.

*"It was for this freedom that Christ set us free [completely liberating us]; therefore keep standing firm and do not be subject again to a yoke of slavery [which you once removed]." Galatians 5:1. Amp Bible.*

Remember, as the scripture revealed earlier in Galatians 5:17, that this period brings about a self-enforced spiritual warfare that prevents you from walking in all that God has for you. It keeps you trapped because whilst the flesh and spirit are warring after each other, you cannot do what you ought to be doing. Well, this is exactly what the enemy would love for the children of God to be doing with their lives. Becoming so entangled again in a yoke of bondage that we allow this warfare to steal the purpose that God has for our lives and to hold us in captivity. But thanks be unto God. Satan is under our feet! And he cannot stop God's plan for His children. We must choose today, in this time, to walk in the purpose and freedom that God truly has for us and has laid out for us by following His Word knowing that it is never too late.

*"For the gifts and the calling of God are irrevocable". Romans 11:29. NKJV.*

Now, if you think that we are saying that all unmarried people should go ahead and marry someone the day after meeting them, then unfortunately, you have completely missed the point. We believe in the blessed purpose of marriage, but we also know that there are some that God has specifically called to be wholly committed to Him in singleness, and that too is a blessing. The apostle Paul teaches that whatever way God has called you to walk, it is a gift from God.

*"For I would that all men were even as I myself. But every man hath his proper gift of God, one after this manner, and another after that." 1st Corinthians 7:7. KJV.*

However, what we do desire to see is a generation that places the purpose before the benefit. The goal before the gain. A generation that moves away from the "let's see how it goes" mindset and walks into the "marriage is our goal, so let's ensure that the foundations are correct and press towards that goal" truth. When the revelation of our purpose was made clear unto us, it completely changed how we walked out the months before the marriage. We had the date set before us, we had our freedom set ahead of us and we were both chasing after the same goal. Imagine the strength, focus and determination that you too shall walk in when you head into the relationship knowing the purpose of what you are heading into ahead of time.

They say that when you know your purpose, nothing can take you away from it. Well, the same applies with this. When you know what God has already laid out for you, you do not need to walk aimlessly searching for a solution whilst falling to get back up again. Rather, you walk with intent and no person nor temptation can take you away from that. Marriage is God-given and is God's intention for His creation, not dating. Marriage was not given unto us as a possibility, rather, it was given unto us for purpose. Amen.

# CHAPTER 12- FINDING THE ONE?

This is something that as a couple we have been asked many, many times. How do you know when you have found "the one"? How do you know it will work out long-term? What if things are not the same in a few years? All of these are very important questions that certainly do require answers, and so, to do that it is equally important that we first establish the foundation. What is love?

Firstly, we will tell you what it most definitely is not. We are living in a generation where everything is based on impulses and feelings. From movies to music and even social media, everything is designed to bring that temporary high that can have you feeling on top of the world. Unfortunately, that same sensation has worked its way into the mindset of people who are entering into relationships also. The whole "falling in love" concept has forced its way through to the top of the agenda. Awaiting that moment where you find yourself "falling so deep in love" that you have no choice but to follow this emotion and act upon it because it is just so overwhelmingly powerful. This is yet another hurdle that has presented itself and acts as a stumbling block for all. Why? Well, it is simple. If you can fall in love without control, then you can just as easily fall back out of it without control also. Under this doctrine, love becomes nothing more than a sensation and acts as the biggest reason as to why relationships/marriages have a much shorter lifespan today in comparison to previous generations.

So then what is love? Like with all things in life, searching the scriptures is always guaranteed to lead you to truth.

*"For God so loved the world, that he gave his only begotten Son, that whosoever shall believeth in him should not perish, but have everlasting life". John 3:16. KJV.*

Do you see it? God so loved this world that He **gave**. Love is not this overwhelming emotion that we cannot control. In fact, it is an act that we **do**. God demonstrated the great love that He has for the entire population of the world by sending His only begotten Son Jesus Christ to be our saviour. Love is a doing thing. When we love someone, we are making a commitment to practise the act of love towards that person regardless of the mood we are in or what has occurred. You see, if love were an emotion, we would never be able to truly mean the vows that we exchange on the wedding day. How can you say "Till death do us part" or "for better or worse" if love is this overwhelming emotion that controls you? That means you would never truly be able to commit your long-term future to one person because you do not know if that emotion will one day decide to get up and direct itself elsewhere, therefore leaving you in a love-less situation that love forced you into in the first place.

We can see how this very concept alone would leave you bouncing from one relationship to another without even giving you a chance to settle. Truth is that the idea of "falling in love" is a fantasy. Love is an everyday practise that we make towards the person that we have decided to make that commitment to. Jesus Christ Himself made it noticeably clear that love is not shown in what you speak or even in what you feel, but love is shown in what you do. In John 14:15 Jesus Christ spoke unto His disciples and said "*If ye love me, keep my commandments.*" We love by practising the action of love towards those who we make the commitment towards.

Now, we would also like to stress the importance of understanding that love is also a choice. Yes, we choose who we decide to make the commitment of love towards. Without a doubt, there are many circumstances whereby God will clearly identify who He has ordained your future spouse to be, as we have both experienced and explained. However, God has given unto us free will and the ability to choose whether we actually follow that path or not. (Note, this free will is not for us to make up our own minds on whether we believe something is right or it is wrong because God's Word has already done that. But God has given free will to all mankind to choose between following after His Word or the wrong path.)

We have just seen how love is an action that we do. Well, does not even life itself show us that we have the free will to choose what we do and do not do? Can you really walk into a shop without making the decision to walk into the shop prior to doing so? Whilst we know first-hand that God has no problem with showing anyone who He has set for them, we also believe that it is up to you to make that choice of obedience. And once again, Jesus Christ Himself teaches us that we can choose who we make that commitment towards.

*"But I say unto you, Love your enemies, bless them that curse you, do good to them that hate you, and pray for them which despitefully use you, and persecute you;" Matthew 5:44. KJV.*

You see, loving someone who hates you or persecutes you is not something that would occur naturally to anyone, but most definitely requires a purposed effort by us all to do. Would the Lord instruct us to do so if it were not possible? or if it were not something that we could choose to do? Never. According to the bible, the evidence is clear for us to know that love is something that we both choose and do. Knowing this then, how could we possibly walk into a relationship with a like-minded person in fear of what could go wrong? It is up to us to continue to show love throughout the entirety of the marriage. Furthermore, it is also our responsibility to choose the person we aim to make that commitment towards. And before we move on, we believe that it is vital that we understand how God's definition of love really does conquer all.

*"4Love suffers long and is kind; love does not envy; love does not parade itself, is not puffed up; 5does not behave rudely, does not seek its own, is not provoked, thinks no evil; 6does not rejoice in iniquity, but rejoices in the truth;*

*7bears all things, believes all things, hopes all things, endures all things." 1st Corinthians 13:4-7. NKJV.*

So, now that we have established a firm foundation, how exactly do you choose?

Firstly, we would like to mention that we believe that you must be able to look past the 'my type' mindset. There is nothing wrong with having an idea of what you personally prefer in a life-partner, however, oftentimes we grow up with a pre-determined idea on what we want our future partner to be like and usually that list is dominated by the physical appearance. Whilst it is important to be attracted to your partner, there are circumstances within marriages that can cause a change in appearance for either one of the people involved i.e., pregnancy for women. Therefore, we cannot allow this to be the main factor which determines whether you become involved with a person or not because when appearances do change, you must have something a lot deeper than that to withstand.

Remember, our God has created us in **His image** from the beginning meaning that we were first created as the spirit man. The bible also demonstrates in Genesis 1 how God gave all dominion and authority over this earth to the spirit man before He even created the soul and body, meaning that it is by the spirit that we are to operate through life. Knowing this then, it is easy for us to understand that the very first thing we must look at when trying to identify whether a person is right for us or not is their heart. We call this the foundation.

*"Be ye not unequally yoked together with unbelievers: for what fellowship hath righteousness with unrighteousness? And what communion hath light with darkness?" 2 Corinthians 6:14. KJV.*

As believers, the most important thing that we should try to identify before anything else is whether you are equally yoked with the other person. Is that person also a bible-believing individual? This is crucial and unnegotiable in our opinion. When you understand that you have been created for God's glory, what fellowship do you have with someone who does not even believe in Jesus Christ? You are both living for two vastly different reasons and where there is light, darkness cannot dwell.

Now, whilst we are here to lead others to Christ Jesus, this should not be used as an excuse to be unequally yoked with someone in a relationship. What you will see is that as the believer you will start to make compromises within the relationship to keep the unbelieving person happy and that will only lead to a complete falling away. Furthermore, how can "the two become one flesh" if both individual parts are pulling in completely different directions? It's impossible. So, ensuring that you are both on the same page in relation to faith in Jesus Christ is the first and most important step.

Secondly, the Word of God has given us crucial direction regarding what we should ourselves be bringing to the table whilst also showing us what we should be looking to find in our partners. Although we believe that all of these things are 100% grown into and developed for both the man and woman within the marriage, it is important that we look for the potential of these things sooner rather than later so that we can identify a) whether we ourselves understand the responsibility of a marriage and b) whether you see that potential in the other person also. Let's begin with the woman's role.

*"22Wives, submit yourselves unto your own husband, as unto the Lord. 23For the husband is the head of the wife, even as Christ is the head of the church: and he is the saviour of the body. 24Therefore as the church is subject unto Christ, so let the wives be to their own husbands in every thing."* Ephesians 5:22-24. KJV.

As the woman, are you/is she able to submit knowing that the husband is the head of the family just like Christ is the head of the church? Are you able to allow him to lead his family or are you/is she someone who wants to challenge that principle? The bible also teaches us in verse 33 of Ephesians chapter 5 that wives are to reverence their husband. That means to have deep respect for your husband. And it is from that place of respect and fear of God that will enable you to submit to the husband and allow him to lead his family in every thing. You know what the husband's role is and you should have enough respect for him to allow him to lead in his role. As a wife, if you prevent your husband from performing his role, not only are you out of the order set by God, but you are causing your husband to fail in his role also.

*"But I would have you know, that the head of every man is Christ; and the head of the woman is the man; and the head of Christ is God." 1st Corinthians 11:3. KJV.*

Now, it is important to note that the woman is not called to be submissive to her boyfriend. Therefore, do not expect her to submit to you before marriage as she will not and should not. So, if you are looking for a clear indicator to see whether a lady can be submissive, then check her submission to the Word. The Word of God is what shapes us and if she is not able to submit to that authority then there is no chance that she will submit to her husband. After all, the Word of God is where a woman finds her role in marriage.

Now, unto the husbands.

Before we dive into any further teachings on the husband's role, we want to show you something that we believe is oftentimes missed in the preceding verses. Notice that there are two especially important elements for the husband as head of the house mentioned in the scriptures that were dedicated to the wives. The apostle Paul exhorts wives to be subject to their own husband in "every thing". That means that it is the responsibility of the husband to lead his household in **every** aspect of family matters. Whether that be finances, decisions, the way in which you raise your children and most importantly your family's walk in Christ. The man is 100% called to lead. We have seen it all too many times, where the woman is left to make these decisions by herself and the husband stays out of family matters in favour of just going out to "earn the bacon". Again, this order is wrong. Husbands are to be the head over all things relating to their family. And the evidence is found further down in the succeeding chapter.

*"And, ye fathers, provoke not your children to wrath: but bring them up in the nurture and admonition of the Lord." Ephesians 6:4. KJV.*

Do you see that? Who did the Word of God just make responsible for the raising of our children? The fathers. Yet today, what we see is less and less fathers in the homes and many organisations trying their hardest to force the male out of the home set-up. Then we wonder why the young people of today struggle so much with authority. Again, this is clear evidence that when we come away from God's divine order, we only succeed in failing.

Furthermore, Paul compares the husband's headship over his house to the headship of Christ over the church and he reiterates the fact that Christ is the saviour of the body (the church). What this illustrates to us is that not only is the husband responsible for the leadership of family matters, but he is also charged with leading his family unto salvation. Meaning that how he lives his life will not only encourage his wife but also their children in wanting to know Christ themselves and grow a strong relationship with Him. In fact, in the book of Titus chapter 1 we see that 2 of the top 3 most important credentials necessary for a man to be considered as eligible as a bishop in the church are directly related to his marriage and upraising of his children. Therefore, the man's actions should always be in fear of God as he has the permanent task of being the shepherd of his sheep and the minister of God in his home.

Now, as if that is not enough responsibility right there, we can now understand the rest of the passage that Paul has directed towards the role of the husband.

*"25Husbands, love your wives, even as Christ also loved the church, and gave himself for it; 26that he might sanctify and cleanse it with the washing of water by the word, 27that he might present it to himself a glorious church, not having spot, or wrinkle, or any such thing; but that it should be holy and without blemish. 28So ought men to love their wives as*

*their own bodies. He that loveth his wife loveth himself. 29For no man ever yet hated his own flesh; but nourisheth and cherisheth it, even as the Lord the church:" Ephesians 5:25-28. KJV.*

Again, we see what God means when He instructs us to love because Christ loved the church so much that He gave Himself for the church. Men, loving your wives requires sacrificing yourself for her. And why wouldn't you? The scripture teaches us that Christ did this so that He could sanctify and cleanse the church and so, if husbands want their wives also to be sanctified and cleansed then there will have to be a willingness to give yourself for her. We also see from the Word of God that just as the church is the body of Christ, the wife is also to be loved as the body of the husband. Just as you would feed your body when it is hungry and put clothes on your back when it is cold, so too are you called to nourish and cherish your wife. The fact that this comparison is made between the woman in marriage and the church highlights just how important God considers every woman to be in every marriage. When we can begin to understand this, then we will truly begin to understand the importance of sanctifying and cleansing her by the washing of the Word.

Now, are you/is he able to understand the responsibility that comes along with marriage? Are you as the man interested in helping your wife develop in line with the Word of God? You see, God has given these principles in His Word to His children for a purpose. This is for our own benefit and to help us make the right decisions.

*"For this is the love of God, that we keep His commandments. And His commandments are not burdensome." 1st John 5:3. NKJV.*

And finally, we as children of God can have the confidence in knowing that when we follow the path laid out for us in God's Word, we shall have good success. After having instructed the church in the direction of the Lord, the apostle Paul makes one thing unmistakably clear to us all.

*"For this cause shall a man leave his father and mother, and shall be joined unto his wife, and they two shall be one flesh." Ephesians 5:31. KJV.*

Notice what the Word of God teaches us here. The apostle teaches us here that it is only **for this cause** that a man and woman should come together in marriage. In other words, under no other circumstances whatsoever should a man and woman even begin to think about marriage. Only when the man is determined to be this kind of husband shown in the scriptures and the wife is determined to be this kind of wife also shown in the scriptures can a man leave his father and mother and join to his wife.

Again, this emphasises the unnegotiable foundation of being equally yoked from the very beginning as if either person is not a follower of Christ before marriage, their desire will not be to become a biblical husband or wife, but instead they will chase after their own fleshly desires. This again will cause the order to be out of sync with God's Word and as the scriptures reveal to us, when you come out of God's divine order, it only leads to destruction. This is what God has designed marriage to look like and through this we can see just how much He cares about marriage and who we should be entering into marriage with.

Whilst there are many scriptures that God has revealed in His Word for our learning in regards to marriage and choosing partners, we have chosen to share these scriptures with you for the purpose of discussing what to look for when choosing to walk in the purpose of marriage. The truth is, all of this has eternally been part of God's perfect plan and when we follow the footsteps that He has laid out for us, it not only allows us to enjoy the fruits of marriage, but it also allows the marriage to be able to withstand the trials that may come because of the solid foundation that it is built upon. This is a lost treasure in the generation of today but is the key to what has caused previous generations to reach milestones such as 50 strong years of marriage.

*"3Through [skilful and godly] wisdom a house [a life, a home, a family] is built, And by understanding it is*

*established [on a sound and good foundation], 4And by knowledge its rooms are filled With all precious and pleasant riches." Proverbs 24:3-4. Amp Bible.*

# CHAPTER 13- THE NECESSITY

Finally, brethren, whilst our experience of the dating period was very much a unique one for our relationship, we know that God brought us through it not only for our deliverance but also so that we could share these experiences and what we have learnt through the experience with the world. We can honestly say that if we knew then what we do know now, our whole experience would have been hugely different. God has provided a pathway for us so that all who hear can head into this period of their walk in Christ knowing what to expect and ultimately how to walk in it without deception. We never had the opportunity to be shown or taught these biblical truths prior to our relationship or marriage but we thank God that by His grace, we can share with you the will of God and what He has ordained for His children.

*"1Now the Spirit expressly says that in latter times some will depart from the faith, giving heed to deceiving spirits and doctrines of demons, 2speaking lies in hypocrisy, having their own conscience seared with a hot iron, 3forbidding to marry, and commanding to abstain from foods which God created to be received with thanksgiving by those who believe and know the truth." 1st Timothy 4:1-3. NKJV.*

You see, God has warned His people that in these last days people will depart from the faith because they will be lured in by deceiving spirits and doctrines from the devil and his kingdom. Notice, one of the two main demonic doctrines that shall come from these deceiving spirits is the **forbiddance of marriage.** Notice also that these demonic doctrines will come from **deceiving spirits.** So whilst it may even seem like a popular idea on the surface of it, we are called to look at the root of it all. This is why Christ said, *"but judge righteous judgement"*. As we have previously stated, God's Word is absolutely invaluable to us as He has given His Word unto us so that we can stand against all the wiles of the devil in the evil day by being made secure in the truth.

We believe that as the lusts of this world become even more evident and enticing in these last days, there has never been a more appointed time for the church to walk in truth and in freedom in every area of our walk with Christ. The church is to stand up and take its rightful place as the chief authority over this land through Christ Jesus our Lord. Jesus Christ came to set the captives free. Not so that we would just ignorantly lead ourselves back into bondage but so that we could walk in that freedom and ultimately let our light shine and cause others to see the glory of our Lord. Opinions are irrelevant, so too are any worldviews. We are to be guided by the Word of God in all walks of life.

"Godly dating" and any form of "dating" is a trap that only leads to one outcome. Many can try and design whatever method they wish, but it will never change the fact that this was never a place that God intended for His children to be in. Now, you may be able to hide the fact that you are fulfilling your fleshly desires or the desires of your mind from the rest of the world, but at what cost and for how long? And if you are reading this and are currently dating and have put marriage on the back burner due to your own desires, we believe that it is important that you understand this next passage.

*"23And he said to them all, If any man will come after me, let him deny himself, and take up his cross daily, and follow me. 24For whosoever will save his life shall lose it: but whosoever will lose his life for my sake, the same shall save it." Luke 9:23-24. KJV.*

Oftentimes we allow our cares and pleasures to become and remain a priority in our lives and unfortunately, that is the very thing that chokes the Word of God out of our lives. The truth is, God is pleased with the heart that is willing to let go of all the desires of this world in order to bring their life into obedience of the Word and truly follow Him. As previously stated, having goals and aspirations are not wrong. However, your desire to follow Christ must be your priority. Remember, Christ instructs us to seek **first the kingdom of God** and all those other things will be added. That is a promise, but do you trust Him enough?

*"29And he said unto them, Verily I say unto you, There is no man that hath left house, or parents, or brethren, or wife, or children, for the kingdom of God's sake, 30Who shall not receive manifold more in this present time, and in the world to come life everlasting." Luke 18:29-30. KJV.*

And so, if we can leave you with any parting comment, it would be this: BE INTENTIONAL WITHOUT FEAR. The apostle Paul teaches us in the book of Romans chapter 8 about walking after the Spirit of God. Now, he is referring to a life that is purposely walking after the things of God. In other words, our flesh has desires and so too does our mind but choosing to walk in the way that God has prepared for us in His word leads to a life full of freedom, fruitfulness and without any bondage. Furthermore, this path truly allows righteousness to be fulfilled. Remember, God is your **Heavenly Father**, and He really does want only the best for His children on this earth. Trust in Him alone. His grace is sufficient. Amen.

# CHAPTER 14- THE PURPOSE

If you are reading this and have not yet accepted Jesus Christ as Lord over your life, we would like to take this opportunity to share the glorious gospel of Jesus Christ with you.

1) The word "gospel" actually means "good news". God has brought good news to the world.

2) Why is the gospel so important?
*"For we must all appear before the judgement seat of Christ; that every one may receive the things done in his body, according to that he hath done, whether it be good or bad."* 2nd Corinthians 5:10. KJV.
As we see through the scriptures, every inhabitant of this world both past and present will stand before the throne of Jesus Christ. You see, God is a Holy God and so there can be no unrighteousness that shall stand in His judgement. The Lord shall judge every person according to that which has been done in this life and God will pour out His wrath upon all who have followed the course of this world and have gone in the way of unrighteousness and have not submitted to the truth. The Lord Jesus Christ is the truth.

3) So, what is the good news? Well… because of His unfailing love and mercy, God through His Son Jesus Christ has already completed all that is necessary to ensure that all inhabitants of this world have the opportunity to be saved from the wrath which is to come.
*"For God so loved the world, that he gave his only begotten Son, that whosoever believeth in him should not perish, but have everlasting life." John 3:16. KJV.*

Though unrighteousness is worthy of the punishment of God's wrath, He in all of His infinite mercy has given unto mankind a means to be made free from the guilty charge of sin.

B) What's more, God has made this marvellous gift of salvation available for **EVERY PERSON** to receive.

*"For the [remarkable, undeserved] grace of God that brings salvation has appeared to all men." Titus 2:11. Amp Bible.*

The bible teaches us that this grace of God came through Jesus Christ and as we see here, this grace also brought salvation for all men. That means that there is not one person on this earth that cannot receive the gift of eternal life. Regardless of age, race, male or female, social status, your past etc. the gift of salvation is available for ALL flesh.

4) Why do all need saving?

*"22Even the righteousness of God which is by faith of Jesus Christ unto all and upon all them that believe: for there is no difference: 23For all have sinned, and come short of the glory of God;"* Romans 3:22-23. KJV.

You see, God is a Holy God. However, all of mankind were born into this world of sin and by this very nature, all have sinned and come short of His glory. This means that all of mankind face the prospect of God's wrath being poured out upon them. The bible also teaches us that God is no respecter of persons which means that there is not one person who receives a pardon for their sins purely because of who they might be on this earth i.e celebrities, charity giver etc. Therefore, because all have sinned and there is no difference between any person born into this world in His sight, God being the righteous judge that He is, has made that same salvation available for ALL through faith in the Lord Jesus Christ.

5) How did salvation come about?
*"And He [that same Jesus] is the propitiation for our sins [the atoning sacrifice that holds back the wrath of God that would otherwise be directed at us because of our sinful nature—our worldliness, our lifestyle]; and not for ours alone, but also for [the sins of all believers throughout] the whole world." 1st John 2:2. Amp Bible.*
Remember, all have sinned. Every single person born into this world. The bible teaches us that the wages of sin is death. Meaning that the only real thing you earn through life outside of Christ, is death. But thanks be to God. Christ Jesus came to earth, and through His death, burial, and resurrection, He paid the full price of sin and made salvation FREELY available. All the debt that the sin of this world has ever accumulated, was placed upon Jesus Christ and has been wiped clear by the sacrifice of Jesus Christ. This is how much God wants **YOU** to be saved. He spared not even His only begotten Son so that none would have to perish because of their sin but instead would be saved through Jesus Christ. Now, because the debt of sin has already been paid by the sacrifice of Jesus Christ, the Father can legally justify all who choose to believe in His Son Jesus Christ.

6) Are there different ways to receive salvation?
*"Neither is there salvation in any other: for there is none other name under heaven given among men, whereby we must be saved."* Acts 4:12. KJV.
Christ Himself said "I am the way, the truth and the life". Notice, He did not say that He is one of the ways or that there are a few options. The truth is, Jesus Christ is the only way that any person can truly receive salvation and outside of Him, there is no salvation.

7) What must I do to receive salvation?

a) *"I tell you, Nay: but, except ye repent, ye shall all likewise perish."* Luke 13:3. KJV.
   The Lord Jesus Christ was so clear about this matter that He even repeated this same point in the same conversation. Repentance is unnegotiable in order to receive salvation. True repentance means to acknowledge that we do indeed come short of God's glory before accepting Christ, and turn away from your old way of thinking and sinful behaviours, in favour of becoming a true follower of Jesus Christ. We were all born into this world of sin, and so it is important to turn away from that to live a changed life which is after the image of Christ revealed in His Word.
b) *"9that if you confess with your mouth the Lord Jesus and believe in your heart that God has raised Him from the dead, you will be saved. 10For with the heart one believes unto righteousness, and with the mouth confession is made unto salvation. 11For the scripture says, "Whoever believes on Him will not be put to shame." Romans 10:9-11. NKJV.*
   You see, it is the Fathers desire that this salvation that grants eternal life is available for ALL in the world to receive. So much so, that He has made it very simple for us all. Because of the finished work of Jesus Christ on the cross and the debt being paid through His blood, faith in the one who has been raised from the dead leads to our right standing with God and the open confession out of our mouth that Jesus is Lord leads to our salvation. With just your mouth and your heart, the gift of eternal life has been made available unto you, but you have to receive it.
   *"Therefore if any man be in Christ, he is a new creature: old things are passed away; behold, all things are become new."* 2nd Corinthians 5:17. KJV.

Finally, before we leave you, we believe that it is so important that you understand the Fathers heart. The truth is God did not just give His only begotten Son because He had no choice. Rather, He gave His only begotten Son to show His unfailing and faithful love towards His creation. There is nothing that you may have said or might have done that could ever make the grace and mercy of the Father of no effect. God knew you from before you even entered into this world.

*"I say to you that likewise there will be more joy in heaven over one sinner who repents than over ninety-nine just persons who need no repentance." Luke 15:7. NKJV.*

*"3For this is good and acceptable in the sight of God our saviour, 4who desires all men to be saved and to come to the knowledge of the truth." 1st Timothy 2:3-4. NKJV.*

The is the Fathers heart. God cares for ALL. He desires for ALL to be saved. He has made salvation available for ALL because He works ALL things according to purpose of His own will. A-men.

www.ingramcontent.com/pod-product-compliance
Ingram Content Group UK Ltd.
Pitfield, Milton Keynes, MK11 3LW, UK
UKHW020416250726
13967UKWH00007B/2669

9 781803 699851